Life in a
Rain Forest Ecosystem

Janey Levy

The Rosen Publishing Group's
PowerKids Press™
New York

Published in 2009 by The Rosen Publishing Group, Inc.
29 East 21st Street, New York, NY 10010

Book Design: Daniel Hosek

Photo Credits: Cover, pp. 3–25 (borders), 27–32 (borders) © Dmitry Savinov/Shutterstock; pp. 6 (top), 7 ©
Paul A. Souders/Corbis; pp. 6 (middle), 10 (top left) © Frans Lanting/Corbis; pp. 6 (bottom), 11 (jaguar), 10
(top right) © W. Perry Conway/Corbis; pp. 8, 11 (agouti), 16, 25 courtesy Wikimedia Commons; p. 9 ©
Ricardo Azoury/Corbis; pp. 10 (bottom), 19 (top) © Tom Brakefield/Corbis; p. 11 (sun) © Sushi/Shutterstock;
p. 11 (Brazil nut tree) © Colin McPherson/Corbis; pp. 11 (earthworm), 22 © Eric and David Hosking/Corbis;
p. 13 (Amazon) © Bettmann/Corbis; p. 14 © Carl & Ann Purcell/Corbis; p. 15 © Wolfgang Kaehler/Corbis;
p. 18 (left) © Kevin Schafer/Corbis; p. 18 (right) © Theo Allofs/zefa/Corbis; pp. 19 (top), 20, 21 (bottom),
26 © Michael & Patricia Fogden/Corbis; p. 19 (bottom) © Ann Sheffield Jacobi/Corbis; p. 21 (top) © Joe
McDonald/Corbis; p. 24 © Envision/Corbis; p. 27 © George D. Lepp/Corbis; p. 28 © Alison Wright/Corbis;
p. 29 © Gerd Ludwig/Corbis.

Library of Congress Cataloging-in-Publication Data

Levy, Janey.
  Life in a rain forest ecosystem / Janey Levy.
       p. cm.
  Includes index.
  ISBN 978-1-4358-0189-9 (pbk.)
  6-pack ISBN 978-1-4358-0190-5
  ISBN 978-1-4358-2997-8 (library binding)
  1. Rain forest ecology—Juvenile literature. 2. Rain forest animals—Juvenile literature. 3. Rain forest
plants—Juvenile literature. I. Title.
  QH541.5.R27L478 2009
  577.34—dc22
                                        2008050732

Manufactured in the United States of America

Contents

Wet and Wonderful Rain Forests

Imagine a forest with thick vines, colorful flowers, and trees taller than a twenty-story building. Picture it filled with butterflies, birds, frogs, and all sorts of animals you won't find anywhere else. That's what a rain forest is like.

As the name suggests, rain forests get lots of rain. There are two main types—tropical and temperate.

Tropical Rain Forests

Tropical rain forests grow in the warm zones near Earth's **equator**. Their temperatures rarely drop below 64°F (18°C) or rise above 95°F (35°C).

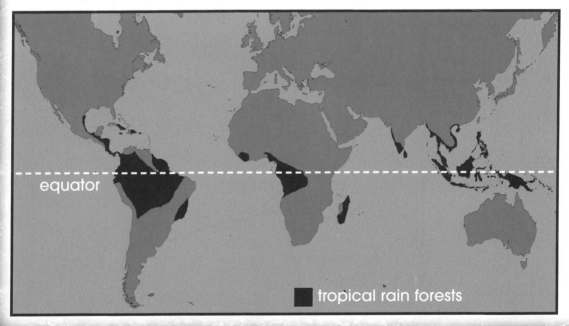

equator

■ tropical rain forests

They receive at least 80 inches (200 cm) of rain annually. The wettest tropical rain forests get more than 33 feet (10 m) of rain in a year!

Temperate Rain Forests

Temperate rain forests are found in cooler regions farther from the equator. Their summer temperatures rarely go above 80°F (27°C), and winter

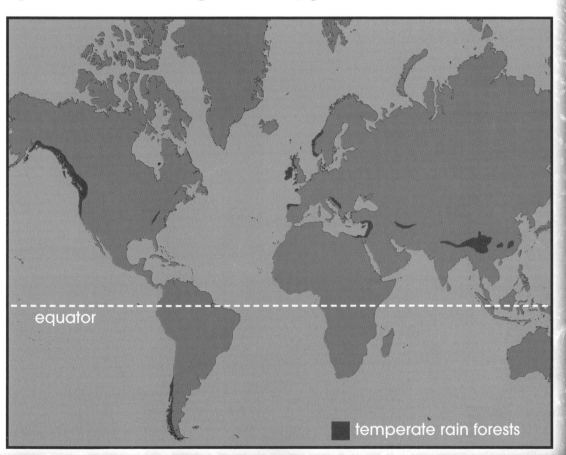

equator

temperate rain forests

temperatures may dip to around 35°F (2°C). They receive about 60 to 200 inches (150 to 500 cm) of rain yearly.

Full of Life

An ecosystem is the community formed by an area's animals, plants, and **environment**. Rain forest ecosystems are found on every continent except Antarctica. Although they cover less than 6 percent of Earth's land, they're home to about half of all plant and animal species on the planet! So what's life like in a rain forest? That's what this book is going to explore. First, however, you need to understand ecosystems and how they work.

frog

butterfly

jaguar

The first rain forests appeared 70 to 100 million years ago. That means they were around at the time of the dinosaurs!

Rain Forest Facts

- About 80 percent of foods we eat—such as oranges, bananas, figs, tomatoes, potatoes, chocolate, cinnamon, and coffee—originally came from rain forests.

- Of the 3,000 plants known to help fight cancer, 2,100 come from tropical rain forests.

- A rain forest park in the South American country of Peru has more bird species than the entire United States.

- A single tree in a tropical rain forest may be home to more than forty ant species.

Ecosystems and How They Work

Every living thing on Earth is part of an ecosystem—including you. Ecosystems can be as large as a rain forest or as small as a pool of water.

Scientists who study ecosystems often focus on how energy flows through them. Energy from the sun is used by plants to make food and is then consumed by animals that either eat plants or plant-eating animals.

Producers, Consumers, and Decomposers

Plants are called producers because they make food in a process called photosynthesis, using the sun's energy, **carbon dioxide** from the air, and

Agoutis are primary consumers related to mice and rats. They're about the size of a rabbit.

water and **nutrients** from the soil. Animals that get the energy they need to live by eating plants are called primary consumers. Animals that eat other animals are secondary consumers. **Organisms** such as earthworms, **bacteria**, and fungi break down dead plants and animals and return nutrients to the soil. They're called decomposers.

The Ecosystem of a Tank Bromeliad

Bromeliads (broh-MEE-lee-adz) belong to a class of tropical rain forest producers called **epiphytes**. Tank bromeliads have leaves that press together at the base to form a "bowl" that collects rainwater. The largest tank bromeliad holds over 2 gallons (7.5 l) of water.

There's not only water in the bromeliad! Tiny bacteria and other organisms break down dead leaves and animals that fall into the water. Larger organisms eat the tiny organisms and are then eaten by even larger organisms, which become prey for still larger animals. A tank bromeliad is a whole ecosystem to all these creatures.

The animals shown here are important secondary consumers in the Amazon tropical rain forest.

ocelot

harpy eagle

anaconda

Food Chains and Food Webs

Producers, consumers, and decomposers make up a food chain. The chart below shows a simple rain forest food chain. Plants and animals in an ecosystem may be part of many food chains. These overlapping food chains make up a food web. Tropical rain forests such as the Amazon rain forest have some of the most elaborate food webs in the world.

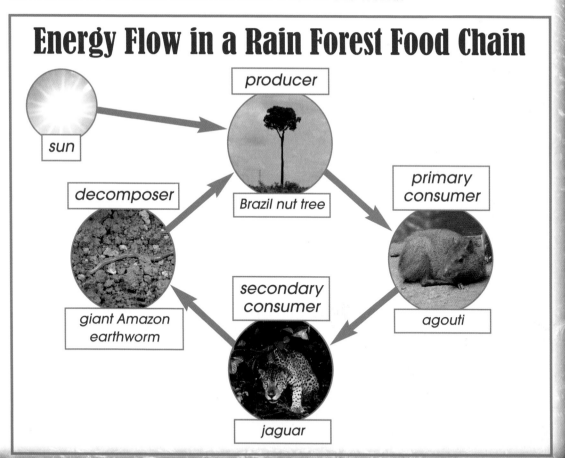

Energy Flow in a Rain Forest Food Chain

sun

producer
Brazil nut tree

primary consumer

agouti

secondary consumer

jaguar

decomposer
giant Amazon earthworm

The Amazing Amazon Rain Forest

Located in the tropics of South America, the Amazon rain forest, or Amazonia, is the world's largest rain forest. It covers over 2 million square miles (5.2 million sq km). Most of it is in Brazil. Parts of it are

also found in countries surrounding northern and western Brazil.

The Amazon River—the world's second longest river—flows through the rain forest and gives it its name. The river carries about 20 percent of all the freshwater in the world. Most of its water comes from melting snow high in the Andes Mountains, which causes the river to flood during the summer. More water comes from the great amount of rain that falls annually—approximately 9 feet (2.7 m)!

The river and forest are home to an astonishing variety of plant and animal species. About 3,000 fish species swim in the river. So far, scientists have identified about 40,000 plant species. The forest shelters hundreds of bird, mammal, amphibian, and reptile species. Scientists have identified about 2.5 million insect species and think there may be almost 30 million still undiscovered!

During photosynthesis, plants take in carbon dioxide and give off oxygen. The Amazon rain forest has been called the lungs of our planet because it produces more than 20 percent of the world's oxygen!

Producers in Amazonia

With 40,000 plant species known so far, Amazonia has plenty of producers. Each layer of the rain forest provides a special home for the Amazon's amazing plants.

The Emergent Layer

The emergent layer includes the tops of the tallest trees—165 feet (50 m) or more in height. Only a few species get this tall, and emergent trees are spaced far apart. The flowers of the towering kapok (KAY-pahk) tree produce **nectar** that provides food for bats, hummingbirds, bees, and wasps.

kapok tree

Brazil nut trees sometimes reach the lofty height of the emergent layer. More often, however, their tops are found just below the emergent layer, in the canopy.

The Canopy

The canopy is home to most of Amazonia's plant and

Because the trees of the canopy form a continuous layer, they don't suffer as much from the strong winds that batter the emergent trees.

animal species. Canopy trees are about 65 to 165 feet (20 to 50 m) tall. In addition to Brazil nut trees, the canopy has Parkia, rubber, and fig trees. Their spreading branches form a roof that blocks most sunlight from the lower layers. Canopy plants provide fruit, nectar, and seeds to many insects, birds, and mammals.

Other plants use canopy trees to help them reach sunlight. Vines called lianas climb the trees and stretch up through the canopy branches. Epiphytes such as bromeliads and orchids grow among the canopy's upper branches.

The Understory and Forest Floor

Only about 2 percent of the sunlight that strikes the canopy reaches the understory, so few plants are able to grow there. Those that do often develop large leaves to absorb as much sunlight as possible or seek sunny spots along the forest's edges or below breaks in the canopy. Cacao trees, orchids, cecropia (sih-KROH-pee-uh) trees, and **heliconia** provide food to numerous insects, birds, and mammals.

Almost nothing grows on the forest floor. Creatures of this zone may feed on fallen nuts, seeds, fruit, and leaves. The stems and trunks of plants that grow to the forest's upper layers provide living spaces as well as sources of food for the forest's animals.

cecropia trees

Layers of a Rain Forest Ecosystem

Layer	What It's Like	Plants	Animals
emergent	• lots of sunlight • very hot • strong wind	• tallest trees, spaced far apart	• eagles and other birds of prey • hummingbirds • monkeys • bats • insects
canopy	• lots of sunlight • home to about 90 percent of rain forest animals	• tall trees • tree branches form roof over lower layers • vines • epiphytes	• insects • snakes • birds • tree frogs • sloths • bats • monkeys
understory	• little sunlight	• young trees • shrubs • ferns • vines • mosses • flowers	• insects • tree frogs • jaguars • anteaters
forest floor	• very dark • covered with dead plants and animals	• few plants	• insects • capybaras • jaguars • ocelots • caimans • agoutis • anteaters

Consumers in Amazonia

Some of the world's most interesting and unusual animals live in the Amazon rain forest. Each forest layer has its own consumers, both primary and secondary.

Primary Consumers

Some primary consumers eat mostly grasses or leaves. The capybara, a larger relative of the agouti, lives on the forest floor and dines mainly on grasses and water plants. In the canopy and understory, three-toed sloths feed mostly on cecropia leaves.

Other primary consumers have more varied diets. High in the canopy, fruit bats feed on flowers and fruits. The canopy is also home to spider

capybaras

fruit bats

red howler monkey

scarlet macaw

monkeys, howler monkeys, and brilliantly colored parrots called scarlet macaws. The monkeys eat fruits, nuts, leaves, and flowers. Scarlet macaws dine on fruits, nuts, and seeds.

The toucan, another canopy bird, eats mostly fruits and berries. However, it isn't strictly a primary consumer. It occasionally eats frogs, lizards, insects, and baby birds.

Secondary Consumers

Not all monkeys are primary consumers. Monkeys called golden lion

tamandua

tamarins are secondary consumers. Their regular diet includes insects and frogs as well as fruits.

Ants form an important part of the diet of many rain forest animals. Giant anteaters, which live on the forest floor, and tamanduas—small anteaters that live mostly in trees—eat mainly ants and **termites**. The small frogs that live in and around tank bromeliads dine on ants and other insects.

Powerful **predators** occupy all the forest's layers. Ocelots and jaguars prowl the forest floor and understory, hunting a variety of mammals, reptiles, and birds. Swarms of army ants kill insects, small lizards and mammals, and even climb trees to kill baby birds in their nests! In the forest's rivers, anacondas and large members of the crocodile family called caimans eat almost anything they can catch. High in the upper layers, green snakes called emerald tree boas and huge harpy eagles feast on birds, lizards, and mammals.

lizard and emerald tree boa

Leaf-Cutter Ants

Amazonia has fourteen species of leaf-cutter ants. You've probably guessed from their name that these ants cut leaves off plants. You might think that means the ants eat the leaves. However, that's not the case. Leaf-cutter ants are actually farmers! They take the leaves to their nests, crush them, and raise fungus on them. That fungus is the ants' food.

21

Decomposers in Amazonia

Eventually, even the tallest trees and fiercest predators die. Decomposers break down the dead plants and animals, returning the nutrients they contain to the soil. Living plants absorb the nutrients, and the energy cycle begins again.

Some decomposers, such as bacteria, are too small to see without a microscope. Others are much larger. Ants and termites are important decomposers in Amazonia. So are millipedes, which resemble worms with lots of legs; some have over 100 pairs of legs! Earthworms also help break down dead matter. You've probably seen plenty of earthworms, but those in Amazonia might surprise you. Some live in trees. The giant Amazon earthworm, which lives in the ground, can be almost 2 feet (60 cm) long!

In Amazonia's warm, moist climate, decomposers work more quickly than they do in other ecosystems. Dead matter is broken down within 6 weeks.

Giant Amazon earthworms are rarely seen above ground.

The Amazon Rain Forest Ecosystem

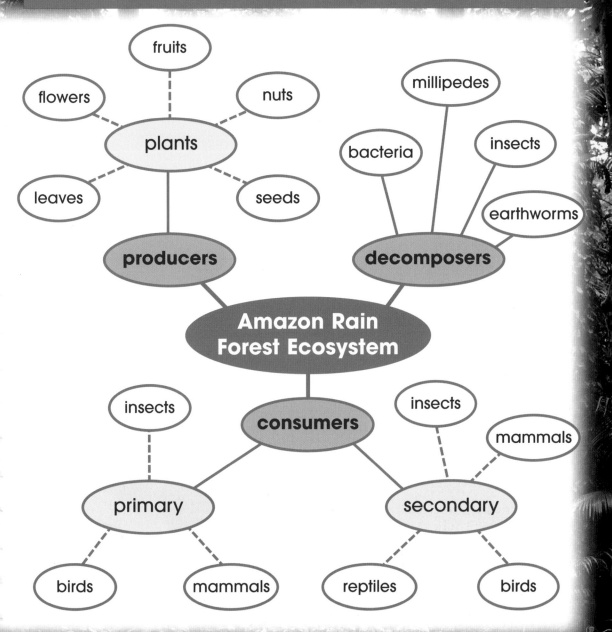

Interdependence and Symbiotic Relationships

Relationships between rain forest organisms aren't always as simple as those between producers, consumers, and decomposers. Some are based on interdependence—which means the organisms depend on each other for survival. A special form of interdependence called symbiosis occurs when two different organisms live in very close association.

Interdependence Between Animals and Plants

Agoutis, Brazil nut trees, bees, and orchids provide one example of interdependence. Agoutis primarily eat Brazil nuts—they're the only animals able to chew through the nuts' outer covering to release the seeds. Agoutis help Brazil nut trees by spreading their seeds throughout the forest. In addition to their dependence on agoutis, Brazil nut trees depend on a single bee species to **pollinate** their flowers. In turn, the bees' survival depends on a certain orchid species.

Brazil nuts

The bees get nectar from the orchid; they also pick up a special scent they need to attract mates.

The relationship between Azteca ants and cecropia trees provides another example of interdependence. The ants live inside the hollow stems of

Orchid bees have long tongues that help them pollinate flowers.

The fig wasp spends most of its life inside a fig and is responsible for pollinating the flowers of the fig tree. Neither the tree nor the wasp can survive without the other.

cecropia trees; a necessary part of their diet is a special juice produced by the trees. In return, the ants chase away insects that may harm the cecropias and kill climbing vines that might choke these trees.

Symbiotic Relationships

Some ant species have symbiotic relationships with certain caterpillar species. The ants feed on sweet juices produced by special spots on the caterpillars' backs. In exchange, the ants protect the caterpillars from attack. Sometimes the ants even take the caterpillars to their nests at night for safety!

Some termite species have bacteria and other tiny organisms living inside them. The termites depend on the bacteria and other organisms to help break down the wood they eat. In turn, the bacteria and other organisms get nutrients and a place to live.

These are only a few examples of interdependence and symbiosis in Amazonia. Such relationships are very common in the rain forest.

Termites, such as those shown here, resemble pale ants. Bacteria in their guts convert the wood the termites eat into sugar.

The Importance of Biodiversity

Have you ever heard the term "biodiversity"? It means the diversity, or variety, that exists among organisms and their environments. Rain forests have the greatest biodiversity on Earth, and that biodiversity is important to everyone.

Biodiversity makes rain forests beautiful, fascinating places. Those qualities are worth valuing. However, rain forests may affect you in a more direct way. Remember those rain forest facts from the first chapter? Here are some more. Tropical rain forests contain at least 3,000 fruits; so far, people outside the rain forests eat only about 200 of them. Scientists have tested less

medicines made from plants

than 1 percent of tropical rain forest plants and have already found that thousands can be made into important medicines. Think how many more foods and medicines might be found!

Remember, too, that rain forests' organisms are linked through interdependence and symbiosis. The loss of one known organism might result in the loss of many that are still unknown. Only by maintaining the rain forests' biodiversity can people preserve both the known and unknown treasures they hold.

There's so much scientists still have to learn about rain forests. In fact, they know more about the ocean floor than they do about Amazonia's canopy.

Protecting Earth's Rain Forests

Rain forests today face many dangers. Pollution harms them. People destroy them to create farmland or harvest the forests' wood. People capture wild animals to sell as pets. Yet there are things we all can do to help save rain forests. Here are a few ideas.

✔ Learn about the ways pollution where you live can harm faraway rain forests, and learn what you can do to prevent it.

✔ Learn what products are created in ways that harm rain forests and refuse to buy or use them.

✔ Support organizations that help protect rain forests.

✔ Write to government leaders about the importance of rain forests.

✔ Tell your family and friends about rain forests and why they're important.

✔ Organize a special event at your school to educate students about rain forests.

Working together, people can help make sure Earth's rain forests flourish for centuries to come.

Glossary

bacteria (bak-TIHR-ee-uh) Microscopic organisms found almost everywhere on Earth. Some cause diseases; others are beneficial.

carbon dioxide (KAHR-buhn dy-AHK-syd) A gas in the air that plants use to make food.

environment (ihn-VY-ruhn-muhnt) The conditions in which an organism lives.

epiphyte (EH-puh-fyt) A plant that gets water and nutrients from the air and grows on another plant without harming it.

equator (ih-KWAY-tuhr) An imaginary line around the middle of Earth that divides it into two halves, northern and southern.

heliconia (heh-luh-KOH-nee-uh) A type of tropical plant with large leaves and bright flowers.

nectar (NEHK-tuhr) The sweet liquid produced by the flowers of many plants.

nutrient (NOO-tree-uhnt) Something necessary for living and growing.

organism (OHR-guh-nih-zuhm) A living creature.

pollinate (PAH-luh-nayt) To transfer a fine dust called pollen from one flower to another to enable the flower to make seeds or fruit.

predator (PREH-duh-tuhr) An animal that hunts other animals for food.

termite (TUHR-myt) A type of small insect related to cockroaches that lives in colonies and eats wood.

Index

Due to the changing nature of Internet links, The Rosen Publishing Group, Inc., has developed an online list of Web sites related to the subject of this book. This site is updated regularly. Please use this link to access the list: http://www.rcbmlinks.com/rlr/rainf